ALL THINGS OWLS FOR KIDS

FILLED WITH PLENTY OF FACTS, PHOTOS, AND FUN TO LEARN ALL ABOUT OWLS

ANIMAL READS

WWW.ANIMALREADS.COM

THIS BOOK BELONGS TO...

_____

_____

WWW.ANIMALREADS.COM

CONTENTS

Welcome to the wonderful world of owls!	1
What Is an Owl?	5
The Most Fascinating Species of Owls	15
The History of Owls	43
Unique Characteristics and Appearance of Owls	53
The Life Cycle of Owls	63
Human Impact on Owls	67
Thank You!	71

WELCOME TO THE WONDERFUL WORLD OF OWLS!

Owls are one of the most unique, mystical, and famous birds in the world. With their distinctive calls, googly eyes, wise expression, and fluffy feathers, owls have been capturing the hearts of young and old alike since the beginning of time.

These magical creatures are known for their insanely flexible necks – you may already know that owls can turn their heads *almost* a full loop around – and their wiser-than-though expression.

Yet, truth be told, owls are even more amazing than the storybooks would have us believe. Exceptional hunters with piercing eyesight, these majestic overlords of the skies boast an array of unique attributes.

Keen to learn more about the formidable owl?

Then join us on our educational flight of fancy, and together, may we discover all there is to know about owls...

The true kings of the night sky!

IT'S

OWL

GOOD!

WHAT IS AN OWL?

Owls are a type of bird from an animal order called **Strigiformes**. *Funny name, right?* Well, this family includes birds that **sit upright** and are most active at night (***nocturnal***). The term 'Strigiformes' comes from an old Latin word meaning 'owl shaped,' so yep, the whole animal family is basically made up only of owls!

More than 200 different species of owls exist on our planet. Although they have a mountain of similarities, they can also differ quite a bit.

Owls are what we call **birds of prey**, which means that they are enthusiastic hunters of other animals. *Oh, but don't worry*: humans, and their pet cats and dogs, are not the preferred lunch of owls. Instead, owls *prefer* to feed on **invertebrates**, which are small animals (like insects, worms, and spiders) that have no backbone.

Phew...we dodged a bullet there!

FUN FACT: It is a common mistake to believe that owls can turn their heads ALL the way around. They can actually turn it about 270 degrees, which is about two-thirds of a full loop. Still, a very impressive thing to do!

WHAT MAKES OWLS SO SPECIAL?

Owls are truly sensational hunters. First of all, their eyesight is out of this world! They have what scientists call **stereopsis binocular vision**. This means they can see the same object with both eyes at the same time and can map out its location, perfectly. *Only owls and a few other birds of prey have this amazing ability!*

Owls also have very **sharp talons**, **superb hearing**, and **noiseless feathers**, which means they are almost **completely silent when they fly**. All of this, combined, helps them surprise their prey and catch it successfully.

Silent flight is the specialty of these birds, which, we are sure you'll agree, is pretty much like having a superpower!

Spending the day resting and the night hunting is what an owl does best. Have you ever heard of the expression *'to be a night owl'*? Yep, that means someone is just like an owl and is much more active after dark!

Owls are mostly **solitary** birds, which means they prefer to live alone *most of the time*. They can live in all sorts of different environments, so they are what you'd call a highly **adaptable** animal. They can adapt anywhere!

In fact, owls are found on every single continent on earth except Antarctica – but, to be fair, Antarctica is such a harsh place that only one bird species is native to the continent!

Now, you know how we said that owls prefer to eat invertebrates? Ok, while this part is true, there is more to the whole owl-feeding story. Although owls prefer to munch on small squishy animals, they have been known to also attack and feed on small mammals like mice and other birds... even birds that are much bigger than themselves!

Some owl species actively hunt osprey (*which are hawk-type birds*), and other species, mainly in Asia and Africa, feed almost entirely on fish!

Hey... we did say owls are very adaptable animals, right?!

HOW DO OWLS PREFER TO LIVE?

Like all solitary animals, owls do come together to make and raise their babies. Moreover, there are a few species of owls that are incredibly sociable and like to live in groups.

FUN FACT: A group of owls is called a **parliament**! Male owls are called **cocks**, female owls are called **hens**, and baby owls are called **owlets**.

Owls are renowned for displaying **sexual dimorphism**. This is a fancy way of saying that their size or other unique differences between the sexes allows us to quickly tell them apart. In the case of the owls, the female is larger than the male, although how much larger really depends on the owl species.

Scientists believe that male owls are smaller because they are the main hunters of the family. A smaller body helps owls fly and hunt better, which is probably why they evolved to be smaller. On the other hand, female owls are meant to stay and guard the nest, so they need to be larger to protect their babies and go a longer time without food. Mama owls usually wait with the kids while dad owls go hunting for food!

Solitary or not, owls really perfect the art of teamwork so they can survive and raise their owlets successfully. **Because we all know that work is always best when shared!**

WHAT DO YOU CALL AN OWL WHO'S BEEN CAUGHT IN THE ACT?

A spotted owl!

THE MOST FASCINATING SPECIES OF OWLS

All up, there are over 200 species of owls in the world, divided into two families: **true (*typical*) owls** and **barn owls**.

Can you tell them apart?

You sure can! True owls have round flat faces with orange or yellow eyes, and most have cute fluff on their ears. On the other hand, Barn owls have heart-shaped faces and dark eyes, with no fluff on their ears at all.

Wanna know who's who, who's who, who's who in the family of owls? **Sorry, we couldn't resist!**

Let's go find us some fascinating owls, shall we?

BLAKISTON'S FISH OWLS

Meet the largest owl species in the world! The Blakiston's fish owl grows a wingspan of a whopping 6.5 feet and may grow up to 28 inches tall. They are not only the largest but perhaps one of the rarest owl species on the planet as well. Only about 2,500 such owls are believed to be left in the world, so they are considered **endangered**.

These majestic birds live in just a few specific areas in the world and, when left unthreatened, can live for up to 15 years. They weigh up to 9 pounds and are a sub-variety of another owl species, the eagle owl, which we'll meet later on. They are found only in China, Russia, and Japan.

You can identify a Blakiston's fish owl by their ear-like tufts as well as their diet of fish. It would be a birdwatcher's dream to see these mysterious and rather majestic creatures in the wild!

When mating season begins, the male Blakiston will sing the first and third note of the mating call, and will await a female responding with the second and fourth note. *Isn't that simply amazing?* They then sing a duet together, and that's how they know they are a perfect match!

FUN FACT: The Blakiston feeds on all sorts of fish, including pike, trout, catfish, and even salmon. In winter, when rivers freeze over, this incredible hunter will instead prey on smaller mammals and even crabs.

ELF OWLS

As the name implies, from the largest, we go to the smallest owl species in the world. Elf owls are teeny tiny owls that only grow up to six inches and weigh about as much as a golf ball. They are among the most adorable owls in the world! You could easily hold one using both of your hands, **although we never suggest you do so.**

Elf owls are true owls with grayish-brown feathers, yellow eyes, and round heads. They are unique because they love to hop around (*just like kangaroos*) and are super good tree climbers. What makes them even more special is the fact that, unlike most owl species, elf owls don't see well in complete darkness. Instead, they rely on their sharp hearing to pinpoint the location of prey.

Because they are so small, the elf owl likes to take over woodpecker holes and other small tree cavities. They are also preyed on by other owls and bigger birds, so they have to be very careful when out in the open.

During mating season, the male elf owl will decorate its tiny nest and gather a small supply of food. Then it will stand by the entrance and start singing its special mating song, **nonstop**, until a female finally arrives for a visit. Hopefully, she'll be enticed to stay with the food offerings, and that's when the mating ritual will finally begin.

FUN FACT: Given the elf owl cannot really fight back, it will always opt to fly away from danger rather than face it. In order to protect its life, the elf owl will 'play dead' when captured by another animal, hoping the predator will then leave it alone!

SNOWY OWLS

Snowy owls are also true owls, and they are distinct due to their, well, *snowy white* feathers. The males are usually entirely white, while females generally have black spots on their wings. They are one of the largest and heaviest owl species, and have extra feathers because their natural habitat is in the Arctic region of North America, Europe, and Asia. Up north, it gets very cold, so the snowy owl needs extra warm insulation. Even the feet of the snowy owls have extra feathers, so it looks like they're wearing winter slippers!

Now that you know that the snowy owl loves to live in snowy areas, it will make sense why they are so very white. It's to camouflage with the surrounding landscapes so it can easily hunt undetected.

The snowy owls can therefore live in open spaces and, due to their impressive size, can hunt larger prey like hares and ducks. When they catch small prey, like mice, they gulp them down whole, in one fell swoop.

FUN FACT: During the summer, the Arctic region has daylight almost 24 hours a day. This forces the snowy owl to hunt by daylight. This makes it one of the rare owl species that are not exclusively nocturnal!

GREAT HORNED OWLS

With its piercing yellow eyes, fantastic head feathers (*that gives them their name*), and aggressive stare, the Great Horned Owl is one of the most impressive and recognizable species in the owl family in North America. Their ferocious hunting skills are legendary and perfectly match their breathtaking appearance.

Great Horned owls are certainly not afraid to hunt larger prey, like skunks, rabbits, and even other large birds. They can fly up to 50 miles an hour at full speed, weigh up to 4 pounds, and have a wingspan of 57 inches. These guys are so tough that they can even match up against falcons when it comes to a fight over prey!

This ability to hunt effectively has made these owls adaptable to any environment, and, true enough, they are one of the most widespread owls today. In the wild, these magnificent creatures are known to live for up to 30 years. The oldest Great Horned owl ever held in captivity lived to be 50 years old.

FUN FACT: In the Americas, the Great Horned owl has the widest distribution of all species of owls and can be found in deserts, cities, and even forests that freeze over the winter. Amazingly, they are not all the same color, nor are they the same size. In fact, their feather colors differ depending on their surrounding environment (this is meant to help them camouflage in the wild). The more north the owls are, the larger they are!

SHORT-EARED OWLS

Short-eared owls are insanely cute and have perhaps the most expressive faces of them all. They always look like they're mad at something! With their adorable fluff on their heads and round-as-a-ball bodies, short-eared owls are easily recognizable. Luckily, they are also quite widespread, so you have a good chance of seeing them flying about. *Well...as long as you don't live in Antarctica or Australia, that is!*

Short-eared owls love flying around meadows and fields, especially at dusk. They're one of the few owl species that nest on the ground, in burrows usually made of tall grass and shrubs. To attract a mate, the male short-eared owl will make whipping sounds by swiftly clapping its wings. Amazingly, owlets will start making high-pitched calls while they are still **IN** their egg and will continue to call out for about a week. After this, their voice will 'soften' to an adorable hoot.

FUN FACT: Short-eared owls travel pretty far and are known to make treks of more than 1,200 miles, which is something many owl species don't do. One particularly courageous short-eared owl was even found landing on a ship right in the middle of the Pacific Ocean, about 700 miles away from the nearest landmass! Crazy travelers, right? This is the main reason the short-eared is one of the few owl species found on remote islands all over the world.

LONG-EARED OWLS

Like the short-eared owls, the long-eared owls are named after their head feathers. In this case, however, their feathers stick up quite a bit. Long-eared owls are known to be very territorial and defensive of their nests, which can make them aggressive.

To intimidate a potential attacker, this owl will spread its feathers in an attempt to appear bigger than it is. To nest, they invade the abandoned homes of other large birds, such as hawks, magpies, or ravens.

What's unique about this species is that once they find another owl to be their partner, they will be partners for life. This makes them **monogamous** birds. Male long-eared owls prepare an entertaining flight display for females to try and attract them.

This medium-sized owl is quite widespread in the Northern hemisphere, which is the top 'half' of our planet. In fact, it is a species of least concern according to animal protection agencies. During harsh winters, the long-eared owls will migrate to southern countries, and it is here they will have their babies.

FUN FACT: The beautiful speckled feathers of this owl is an amazing protective adaptation. When there are babies in its tree nest, the adults will cover the entrance with their bodies and spread out their wings to try to camouflage the nest.

SCREECH OWLS

A small owl species that grows only to about 10 inches in height, the screech owl has an unusually large head compared to the rest of its body. It also features a yellow beak and gorgeous white eyebrows. It can come in two colors (*grey or red*) and, unlike its name would suggest, it does not screech at all.

These owls are known for their brilliant camouflaging skills, which helps keep them safe, especially during the day when they are mostly sleeping. They blend right into a hollow tree, and no one would even notice that they are there!

Since they come in different shades, they have become really good at selecting nests within trees that match their feathers. *Isn't that pretty clever?*

FUN FACT: Sometimes, a screech owl will use a snake to clean up house! If their nest is infested with small parasites, a screech owl will pick up a snake and deliver it to the nest so it can clean it up!

EAGLE OWLS

All owls are special, but some think that Eagle owls are a cut above the rest. Their scientific name is bubo bubo, which is a lot more fun to say if you ask us.

Eagle owls actually do look like eagles, thus their name. They are found throughout Europe and

Asia and are often called Eurasian Eagle owls for this reason. Eagle owls are famous in the owl family because they have no natural predators. That is, there are no other big birds or animals that actively hunt them for food. This makes them **apex predators** and is also why they can live up to 20 years old.

Some say that if they live a pampered captivity life, they may live for up to 50 years! They are also pretty large and have a wingspan of six feet, challenging their cousins, the Blakiston's fish owls, in this regard.

Their bright orange eyes and wicked feather *'hairdo'* make these among the most distinctive species of owls.

FUN FACT: Eagle owls prefer rocky landscapes, and males will select remote rock crevices and steep cliffs to create a nesting home for their partner and future babies.

BURROWING OWLS

Burrowing owls are one of the smartest owls out there, preferring to live underground and decorating their living quarters with dung (*you know...poop!*), so they can attract their favorite meal, *the dung beetle*. We know it might sound a little stinky, but when you think about it, it's actually quite genius!

Burrowing owls are small but feisty. This is definitely one owl you wouldn't want to mess with. Aside from burrowing their own tunnels, these clever owls will also 'steal' burrows from other animals, including turtles, so it's considered a bit of a bully in the owl world. But hey, *an owl's gotta do what an owl's gotta do to survive!*

FUN FACT: The burrowing is the only owl species that nests underground and doesn't live in trees. It also hunts during the day and sleeps at night which is super uncommon among owls. One more thing that's interesting about them is that they're pretty sociable owls and can often nest in a little underground community. When surprised or threatened, the burrowing owl will flatten itself on the ground (hoping it is not seen) rather than fly away!

BARN OWLS

Last but not least, barn owls are perhaps the most famous owl of all time. If you see owls in the movies or cartoons, it's most likely a barn owl.

Known for their distinct heart-shaped faces and piercing eyes, barn owls come in many different colors. The peculiar shape of their faces enables them to hear noises from afar. *How far, you ask?* **Very far!** They might actually hear you talking or reading this book out loud right now!

Oh no, we're not exaggerating. *All right, maybe a little bit.*

Apart from excellent hearing, barn owls also have superb vision, but they prefer to hunt using the former. They are always seen hunting for rodents on open fields, flying back and forth swiftly.

Although quite large, barn owls weigh next to nothing! They are about the size of a cat but only weigh around a pound.

Barn owls are the most widespread of all owl species, found almost anywhere in the world. In fact, they're considered one of the most common of all bird species around the world.

FUN FACT: *So, do barn owls really love to live in barns?* In fact, they do! Isolated barns in the midst of fields are the ideal place for this owl to live, and that's precisely where it got its name. Protected from the weather and other predators but having fields of delicious prey at their **talon** tips, *barns make the ideal home for these clever birds.* Farmers love them, too, because they are an excellent and very organic form of pest control! Of course, this doesn't mean they *only* live in barns. Barn owls can easily make themselves at home in all sorts of 'holes'... including chimneys!

OWL-WAYS

CHILLING!

THE HISTORY OF OWLS

Where did owls come from? Did they evolve from another species? Were there already owls on our planet millions of years ago? **You're no doubt wondering about the history of the owl!**

Let's find out where these incredible birds came from...

The history of owls is actually shrouded in mystery. Owls have always been a part of ancient stories like epics and fables, so we know that they play a significant role in the history of the world. But these stories refer to a time that is quite recent.

What about millions of years ago? Were there owls then too?!

Scientists say that owls are a part of the group **Telluraves**. The same group includes vultures, hawks, cuckoos, kingfishers, woodpeckers, parrots, and a few other bird species still living today.

It is said that owls were already present on our planet 60 to 57 million years ago, or at least one of their ancestors was. So yes, they actually lived with the dinosaurs! *And, they survived the asteroid that led to the extinction of those gigantic reptiles.*

Because of this, owls are known as **the oldest land birds ever!**

It's also true that many other owl species went extinct as time passed, which makes sense because we only have true owls and barn owls living today.

Owl species are found in various parts of the world, so that means that they were already widespread even in ancient times. This shows that owls are one of the most adaptable birds on the planet and that adaptability helps them survive the many challenges they face to this day.

If you survived multiple extinction events, then boy, **you are a true survivor in the animal world!**

FUN FACT: Dinosaurs lived on our planet about 65 million years ago. They lived during an era called the **Cretaceous period.** Dinosaurs roamed our planet for about 165 million years. Based on geological evidence, dinosaurs went extinct when an asteroid struck the earth. They say that birds are dinosaurs. *So, maybe, could it be that owls are descendants of small dinosaurs that survived the asteroid strike?*

ANCIENT BELIEFS AND OWLS

Let's talk about what ancient people thought about owls now that we're talking about history.

It turns out that people from different corners of the world have different opinions on what owls really are and what they stand for.

The Japanese think owls are symbols of good luck, and they actually carry owl charms with them to keep them lucky. But, in Africa, most specifically in Kenya, it's the complete opposite. Kenyans think that owls bring poor health and bad luck, so they steer clear of them and all their symbols.

In the West, most specifically in Europe, owls are regarded as symbols of wisdom. *Are you familiar with Greece?* The ancient goddess of Greece, called Athena, has the owl as her symbol, since owls represent higher intelligence.

In India, owls represent wealth and prosperity, meaning they bring fortune into people's lives. And lastly, in Native American culture, owls are known to bring danger. That's why adults in that culture tell naughty kids that the owls will come and get them if they don't behave.

What about you? What do you think owls represent in your culture?

It is pretty amazing to learn the same animal can have such amazing meaning in so many different cultures around the world.

ARE OWLS CLOSELY RELATED TO ANY OTHER ANIMALS TODAY?

We mentioned a bunch of birds earlier that may have shared the same ancestors as owls. But there is one specific bird species living today that is said to be the closest relative of owls: the **nightjar**.

Nightjars are nocturnal birds and are, much like owls, also found all over the world. They have long wings, short legs, and shorter than usual bills. They primarily eat insects, that's why they are also known as bug eaters. These birds do look eerily like owls, and, in fact, the two are often mistaken for one another.

Nighthawks are also birds from the same family of nightjars, and they are also closely related to owls.

WHEN DOES AN OWL GO, "MOOOOOO!"

When it's learning a new language!

UNIQUE CHARACTERISTICS AND APPEARANCE OF OWLS

Owls usually have **forward-looking eyes** and have **acute vision and hearing**. Their eyes don't move from side to side (*weird, right?*), which is why the owl has developed the ability to move its head around to such a huge extent. Interestingly, owls are actually farsighted, which means they can't see things that are very close to them. That's why they hunt safely from afar!

All this makes owls excellent hunters, especially after dark. Their **beaks** are sharp and hooked on the end, which is how you can tell a bird eats (and tears) meat.

An owl's feathers aren't just there to make it look pretty, of course. The feathers are there to protect them from extremes in temperature (that's why northern species have more of them), and the head feathers, in particular, are shaped to help deliver sound effectively to their ears. This works masterfully when they need to spot prey but also when they need to keep an eye out for predators of their own.

We probably don't need to tell you why owls have such sharp talons, right? Yep, you guessed right, those pointy curved nails help them kill and capture prey!

Amazingly, owls don't usually drink water. Instead, their thirst is satisfied by drinking the bodily fluids of their prey. **Yikes!**

What's even more surprising is learning that owl ears aren't lined up with one another. This makes them asymmetrical. Why? So they have a wider range of hearing than normal!

WHY ARE OWLS NOCTURNAL?

Hunting at night is a very common attribute for many animals around the world. Aside from owls, other nocturnal animals include bats, foxes, hedgehogs, badgers, and most big cats.

These animals have all evolved to be nocturnal for many reasons related to their survival. During the nighttime, hunting for food is much easier. Sure, it's darker, but to nocturnal animals, it's a chance to avoid the sun's heat. There's also less competition for food at night, and it's relatively safer from predators.

Nocturnal animals have evolved to improve their physical traits to be more adaptable for hunting after dark. And it's not just hunting, owls and other nocturnal animals do all sorts of activities during the night.

There are only three known **diurnal** owls (meaning they are active **during the day**). These are the burrowing owls we met earlier, as well as the northern pygmy owls and the northern hawk owls.

Animals like owls are also known for having a superb sense of hearing, aside from excellent night vision. Some nocturnal animals also develop a keen sense of smell, something that's way better than that of humans. *Not owls, though.* Owls aren't necessarily known to have a good sense of smell. That's at least one thing that owls aren't really good at. But their other abilities sure make up for that one weakness!

FUN FACT: Owls are very clever indeed and will only lay eggs when their food is plentiful. During a drought of prey, they will lay fewer eggs, so they have less food they need to gather for their growing babies.

These sure are some of the smartest animals around.

WHERE DO OWLS PREFER TO LIVE?

Given owls are so adaptable, it probably won't surprise you to know that owls can live happily in all sorts of habitats.

Owls can be found in wooded areas, grassy plains, rainforests, and even deserts. They live in trees, hollow logs, holes in the ground, abandoned nests of other birds, barns, and even inside cacti.

FUN FACT: Unlike many other birds, owls do not build their own nests! Instead, they take over the nests of other birds or the living quarters of other species. *Does that make them super lazy or just super-duper smart?* **You decide!**

Normally, owls don't spend much time on top of trees like so many other birds do. If you happen to see an owl on top of a tree, you can bet he or she is stalking its next lunch victim.

Yet given they spend their days asleep, owls need to find perfect sleeping spots that are hidden and protected from other predators. That's why they love taking over nooks and hidden crannies where they can fit and camouflage.

Owls really do love living in barns and urban areas. It's not unusual to find owls in abandoned houses or buildings. It's also not uncommon to find an owl staring right at you from outside your window!

For some curious reason, owls are not known to be afraid of people. This is probably because they have never been actively hunted by humans (*thank goodness!*) On the contrary: owls are super defensive when it comes to their young, and if people get too close, they have been known to lash out and attack to protect their babies. *A pretty natural response, right?* **That's why it's important to always admire owls from afar.** You just never know if there are babies nearby or if you are mistakenly acting in a way that makes the owl feel threatened. They have sharp talons after all, so best steer clear and simply admire them from a respectful distance.

WHERE HAVE YOU BEEN OWL NIGHT!

THE LIFE CYCLE OF OWLS

On average, owls living in the wild and across all species will live to about nine to ten years of age. Owls that live in captivity may live longer, to around 30 years old.

Why is that so, you're wondering? Because owls in captivity are protected from the elements that may harm them in the wild such as predators, accidents, or diseases.

The life cycle of owls has four stages: **egg, chick, owlets**, and onwards to **adulthood**.

Owls lay about two to twelve eggs per year, and mama owls lay on them to keep them warm and make sure they are safe. Meanwhile, it's the role of the papa owls to look for food to feed her. After about a month, chicks will pop out of the eggs. They will instinctively scrape their way out of their shells to completely emerge.

At this point, it is the hen's job to tear food to pieces and feed all of her babies. As the chicks grow bigger, they become owlets but are still dependent on their mamas to feed them until they turn 12 weeks old.

At three months of age, owlets are ready to leave the nest and can now fly well enough to look for their own food. When an owl is about 9 to 12 months old, they are considered adults.

Soon enough, these owls will be ready to find their own partner to start the cycle of life once more.

FUN FACT: Almost all owl species are monogamous, which means they find **ONE** mate and stay with them for life. The other famous birds who are deeply monogamous is the penguin!

YOU ARE

HOOTIFUL

HUMAN IMPACT ON OWLS

Unfortunately, though, owls are often victims of human impact nonetheless. Being such secretive and shy animals means we often don't realize our actions can have a negative effect on local owl populations. Owls have been known to be accidentally poisoned (*say, when we try to poison worms or pests in our gardens*), or they lose their homes when we cut down a lot of trees in forests.

Owls can also get hit by cars at night (when they are low flying in search of prey), and they sometimes get electrocuted on power lines.

Aside from vehicle accidents, the most impactful human activity is using chemicals in agriculture. By using too many strong chemicals, we are poisoning owls (*and other birds*) by poisoning the worms and small animals they feed on.

Luckily, there are conservation networks all over the world dedicated to educating people and protecting owls.

Perhaps, you'd like to be a part of this amazing movement?

If you do, visit the webpage of the **International Owl Society** (https://www.international-owl-society.com/), so you can learn more about the fantastic projects they run.

THANK YOU!

Thank you for reading this book and for allowing us to share our love for owls with you!

If you've enjoyed this book, please let us know by leaving a rating and a brief review wherever you made your purchase! This helps us spread the word to other readers!

Thank you for your time, and have an awesome day!

For more information, please visit:

www.animalreads.com

THANKS FOR <u>OWL</u> YOU DO!

© Copyright 2022 - All rights reserved Admore Publishing

ISBN: 978-3-96772-121-8

ISBN: 978-3-96772-122-5

Animal Reads at www.animalreads.com

The content contained within this book may not be reproduced, duplicated or transmitted without direct written permission from the author or the publisher.

Under no circumstances will any blame or legal responsibility be held against the publisher, or author, for any damages, reparation, or monetary loss due to the information contained within this book. Either directly or indirectly.

Published by Admore Publishing: Gotenstraße, Berlin, Germany

www.admorepublishing.com

www.ingramcontent.com/pod-product-compliance
Lightning Source LLC
LaVergne TN
LVHW020141080526
838202LV00048B/3986